DECODABLE BOOK 26

Orlando   Boston   Dallas   Chicago   San Diego

Visit *The Learning Site!*

www.harcourtschool.com

D0067226

Printed in the United States of America

ISBN 0-15-327352-6

15 179 10 09 08 07

Ordering Options
ISBN 0-15-323767-8 (Collection)
ISBN 0-15-327353-4 (package of 5)

Contents

Rabbit
and
Mole

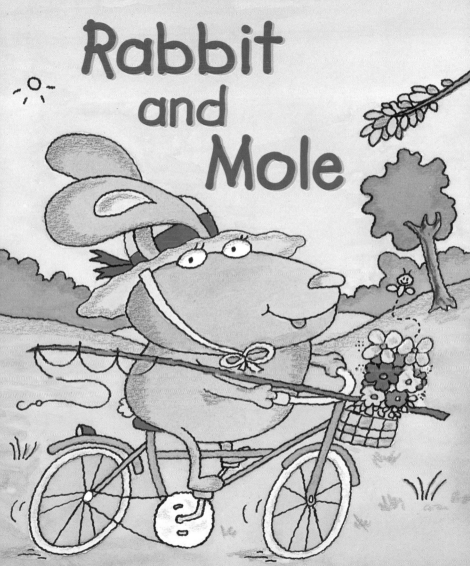

by Kathleen McKinnon
illustrated by Stan Tusan

Mole sent a note to Rabbit.
When Rabbit got home, she
found the note.

Dear Rabbit,

Meet me at the cove.
Bring your fishing
pole.

Your pal,
Mole

Rabbit rode to the cove. She poked
her nose into Mole's hole. He was
snoring!

4

"Mole!" Rabbit called. "It's time to wake up. Did you forget your note?"

"Rabbit!" Mole cried. "I'm glad you
woke me up. Grab your fishing pole.
Let's get lunch."
6

Rabbit sat on a big, flat stone and fished. Mole made a fire. The smoke rose and swirled in the sky.

The friends sat in the grove by the cove. It was a great day!

A Vole Finds a Home

by Becky Gold • illustrated by Doug Bowles

What is this animal? It's a vole.
Voles are field mice.

Voles make nests in holes.
This vole pokes its nose
out of its home.

What is a vole's home like?
It's crowded! Space is close.

When a vole grows up, it's time to make its own nest.

This vole is looking for a home.
It stops to eat. Voles like seeds.

14

The vole pokes its nose in a hole.
It digs past a stone and wiggles in.

Sniff, sniff. What's that?
Another vole! How nice!

Rabbit and Mole

Word Count: 110

High-Frequency Words

day	to
friends	was
great	you
into	your

Decodable Words*

a	forget	let's	**rose**
and	found	lunch	sat
at	get	made	sent
big	glad	me	she
bring	got	meet	sky
by	grab	**Mole**	**smoke**
called	**grove**	**Mole's**	snoring
cove	he	**nose**	**stone**
cried	her	**note**	swirled
dear	**hole**	on	the
did	**home**	pal	time
fire	I'm	**poked**	up
fished	in	**pole**	wake
fishing	it	Rabbit	when
flat	it's	**rode**	**woke**

*Words with /ō/o-e appear in **boldface** type.

A Vole Finds a Home

Word Count: 91

High-Frequency Words

another	of
are	to
finds	what
looking	what's

Vocabulary Word

field

Decodable Words*

a	it	sniff
and	its	space
animal	it's	**stone**
close	like	stops
crowded	make	that
digs	mice	the
eat	nest	this
for	nests	time
grows	nice	up
hole	**nose**	**vole**
holes	out	**voles**
home	own	**vole's**
how	past	when
in	**pokes**	wiggles
is	seeds	

*Words with /ō/o-e appear in **boldface** type.